How to Design An Effective Corporate Strategy

Hiriyappa. B, Ph.D.

Contents

Chapter 1 Corporate Strategy
Chapter 2 Corporate Strategy Formulation Implementation Process
Chapter 3 Long Term Objectives and Qualities
Chapter 4 Michael Porter's Generic Strategies
Chapter 5 Grand Strategies Structures in Enterprise's
Chapter 6 Diversification

CHAPTER 1
CORPORATE STRATEGY

INTRODUCTION

Corporate strategy is the design framework of the firm growth and development. Its main objectives are the growth of the company business in a particular direction, extent, pace and timing. Generally, Corporate strategy involves the design objectives, implementation, control of the objectives of firms which are helpful for growth of companies. It determines the company's mission, vision and long term development and growth of firms. Corporate policy depends on its corporate strategy management will be made by strategist of the company.

NATURE, SCOPE AND CONCERNS OF CORPORATE STRATEGY

Corporate strategy is basically concerned with

the choice of businesses, products and markets of the company's. Nature, scope and concerns of corporate strategy as outlined below:

It can be involved and viewed with objectives designed framework strategy of the firm. A strategy designed framework is filling the firm's strategic planning gap.

Actually, it is concerned with the different choice of the firm's products and markets. It generally involves the changes/ additions/ deletions in the firm's existing product market postures in businesses. It serves the customers' needs and requirements and meets and serves the business requirement.

It's able to ensure that the right fit to businesses and how to achieve between the firm's and its business environment.

It helps and focuses to build up the relevant competitive advantages for the firm's in the market. Both corporate objectives and corporate strategy bring together and describe the firm's business concepts.

WHAT DOES CORPORATE STRATEGY ENSURE IN FIRM'S BUSINESSES?

Corporate strategy first time ensure that the firm's business growth and correct alignment of the firm's and its environment. It's ready to serve and ensure that the design strategy which for filling the strategic gaps in business.

It helps and serves to build up the firm's relevant competitive advantages, its primary strategy ensures that the masterminding and working out the right opportunity which fit between the firm and its external environment.

Corporate strategy purposefully firm's weakness converts into strengths and threats converts into opportunities in this way ensure to firm's businesses.

It ensures that responding the environment is part and parcel of a firm's existence in the market. It ensures to arise a major question which is better and how to methodical to response to firm's. Corporate strategy is the opposite of adhoc responses to the changes in the environment in competition, consumer tastes, technology and other variables in firms. It definitely involves the amounts is to long- term, well thought out and prepared responses to the various forces in the business environment.

STRATEGY IS PARTLY PROACTIVE AND PARTLY REACTIVE

The company strength's strategy is typically a blend in the following circumstances:

Proactive actions on the part of managers and responsibility to improve the company's market position and financial performance.

It needed reactions to unanticipated developments and fresh market conditions in the firm's businesses.

The biggest portion of the firm's current strategy flows from previously initiated actions like experiences, resources, strengths, and competitive capabilities along with business approaches. These are working well enough to merit continuation and newly launched managerial initiatives to strengthen the overall position and performance in terms of growth rate and market share of firm's. These things are involved in management game plans. It is deliberate and proactive. It's standing the product of firm's product and services management analysis and strategic thinking determine about the company's situation analysis and its conclusion about how to position the company in the market place and how to tackle the task of compensating for buyer patronage.

A Company's Actual Strategy Is Partly

Planned and Partly Reactive: Actual company strategy involves the Company experiences, know how, Resources, Strengths & weaknesses, and competitive capabilities.

Every strategic movie is not the result of proactive plotting and deliberate management design. Things are happening in firm which cannot be fully anticipated or planned in firms. When the market and competitive conditions of the firm will take either unexpected turn or some aspect of a company's strategy hits stone wall. Some kind of strategic reaction or adjustment is required for companies. Therefore, a portion of the company's strategy is always developing the project. It is coming as a reasoned response to unforeseen developments in the form of fresh strategic maneuvers on the part of rival firms in the market. These are shifting customer requirements and expectations to new technologies and market opportunities which are suitable to be changing political or economic climate or other unpredictable or unanticipated happenings in the surrounding environment. But apart from adapting the strategy which has to changes in the market. And also a need to adapt strategy in terms of new learning emerges. It is pieces of the strategies which are working well with firm and which aren't and as management hits upon new ideas for improving the strategy. Crafting a strategy involves stitching together either a proactive or intended strategy and then adapting first one piece and then another as circumstances that surrounding the company's situation change or better options to emerge as a reactive / adaptive strategy.

DEALING WITH STRATEGIC UNCERTAINTY

Strategic uncertainty is representative of the future uncertain trend or event which has unpredictable in real business. Information gathering and additional analysis in firm's will not able to reduce the uncertainty. Scenario analysis is basically acceptable uncertainty in business. The scenario can be used driven description of two or more future scenarios. Each uncertain require a suitable strategy to make into certainty in the firm's business.

Strategic uncertainty is the strategic implications of strategic managers. It is a key construct in strategy formulation.

External analysis will be emerged with so many of strategic uncertainties to company's. Uncertainties can be managed; these can be grouped into logical clusters or themes.

Strategic uncertainty is useful and assesses the

importance of each cluster in order to set problems with regard to relevant and appropriate information gathering and analysis.

Suitable strategic decisions help to strategist in gathering information, analysis of uncertainties in businesses. Changing conditions of uncertainty, strategist can form a suitable strategy for changing the context of uncertainty of business.

IMPLICATIONS OF STRATEGIC UNCERTAINTY

Each strategic uncertainty involves potential trends or event which can be impacted on present, proposed and even potential strategic business units of company's. Impact of strategic uncertainty will be depended on the strategic business unit of a firm.

Some of strategic business units in a firm which more important to compare to other units in strategic business units. Established strategic business units may be indicated in terms of associated of sales, profits and costs of products and services.

Sales, profits and cost of products and services may not reflect the true value of a firm.

Information needed areas are affected several strategic business units of company's.

Strategic uncertainty implications are to be relevant to impact on strategic uncertainty.

CHAPTER 2

CORPORATE STRATEGY FORMULATION IMPLEMENTATION PROCESS

INTRODUCTION

Corporate strategy formulation–implementation process is the main task of the strategist to frame and implement strategy.

The Stages of Corporate Strategy Formulation – Implementation Process

Craft and executing strategy are the heart and soul of managing a business enterprise. Crafting and executing a company formulation's strategy has involved the five stages of the management process as outlined below:

Developing a strategic vision as concerned

with company's future products and services which based on customer – market-technology.

Setting objectives and using them as a yardstick for measurement the company's performance and progress relating to present and future.

Crafting a strategy to achieve the desired outcomes and move the company along with the strategic discipline which management has charted.

Implementation and executing the selected strategy efficiently and effectively discharge in the company.

Monitoring, developments and initiating corrective adjustments towards the company's long term direction, objectives. Strategy or execution in light of the company's actual performance.

Stage 1: Developing a Strategic Vision
Strategic vision is the future of the company's products, services, market, customer and technology. These are focused to improve its current market position and its future prospect.

It must be determined the proper directional

path the company and should take changes in the company's product and services.

Strategic manager in company carefully draw and reasoned to make conclusions about how to try to modify the company's business and market position in business.

Top management's views and conclusions about the company's attribute towards the products, services, customer, market and technology, these are focusing and constitute a strategic vision for the company.

A strategic vision defines management aims and aspirations for the business and points an organizing in a particular direction path towards the strategic path for identifying the current trends and estimation of the future trends towards the company's business.

Clear and well defined strategic vision ready to communicates management 's aspirations to stakeholders and it helps to guide and encourage energies of company personnel in a common direction.

Mission and Strategic Intents
Strategic managers should be clearly know about their role and responsibilities to company, these are expressed in terms of statement of mission.

Mission and strategic intents are very important both external stakeholders and others managers in the company's.

Mission statements clearly defined and it should accomplish by strategic managers in firms. Mission statements intents is not concerned with the details of strategic business unit competitive strategy or the directions and methods the businesses, it will be taken to achieve a competitive position rather, the concern of firm's overall directional strategic decision.

Strategic managers of a subsidiary will be responsible for changing and developing a strategy for business. While definitions of strategy should be clear and it fit into the firm's subsidiary business and the entire group.

Hamel and Prahalad have highlighted the importance of clear strategic intent can go much further in the business and activities are listed below:
It can be provided with motivation and galvanize along with enthusiasm throughout the organization.
It is providing what they call a sense of density and discovery in business.

When the absence of these, there is risk of different parts of the organization in terms of different levels of management, all members of the organization, it should be pulling in different directions in the firm's activities.

Decisions are a major part of the overall mission in a major corporation, it will exercise constraints elsewhere in business activities. The corporation aspires to earn short-term profits or long-term growth; its focus on selected countries corporation ready to make an investment, particularly in internal innovation use and develop the new products, or the acquisition of the other businesses. For this purpose, to develop strategic choice with regard to strategic matter explicit and it can help to make strategic decisions.

Stage 2: Setting Objectives
Setting objectives play a magnificent role in development and designing of the company mission and vision. Basically, they represent the quantum of growth in this way seeks and achieve in the given time frame. It also endows the company features, products, services, and its characteristics that ensures the projected the growth. Objectives are setting the process, and also tackling the environment and deciding to appropriate

objectives in business.

The objectives provide the basis for major decisions of the firm and also said the organizational performance to be realized at each level at each level.

The main purpose of the setting objectives is to convert the strategic vision into specific performance targets such as results and outcomes of the management in the company. Setting objectives are yardsticks for tracking the company's progress and performance.

Setting objectives is the specific tool for truly stretching an organization to reach its full potential core capabilities.
Company objectives should be improving the financial positions, economic positions and business positions.
Company objectives are to be more intentional and focused on actions.
The objectives are short term and long term objectives which are supported for business enterprise.

The Balanced Scorecard Approach
It is a combination of strategic and financial objectives of the company. It measures the company performance for this purpose, it is required for setting both types of financial and strategic objectives and tracking their

achievement.

The strategic manager takes more care and design the strategic objectives than on achieving financial objectives in business.

Stage 3: Crafting a Strategy to Achieve the Objectives and Vision

Crafting a strategy to achieve the objectives and vision is the third stages corporate strategic process in strategic management.

A company's strategy is at full power only when it's processed from the corporate level to the business level and then from the business level to the functional level and operating levels in firms.

Middle level and Frontline managers cannot do good strategy making without understanding the company's long-term direction and higher level strategies apart from the vision and mission of the company.

Strategy makers in a company belong to the same team and involved in many different pieces of the overall strategy crafted at various organizational levels that need to be in sync and united.

Achieving the unity is the basic tools in strategy making and it is partly a function of

communicating the company's basic strategy, this theme effectively across the whole organization and establishing clear strategic principles and guidelines for lower level strategy that helpful in making strategy at lower levels in the company.
Cohesive strategy making down through the hierarchy becomes easier to achieve when company strategy is distilled into pithy, easy to grasp terminology that can be used to drive consistent strategic action throughout the company.

The greater amount of company's strategic personal who knows, understanding and make to the company's basic direction and looking for strategy, it is the smaller the risk that people and organization units will go off in conflict strategic directions towards crafting strategy and achieve the mission and vision of the company.

Many strategic people are given a strategy making role when strategic decision making is pushed down to Frontline levels.

Good communication of strategic themes and guiding principles of among themes members, thus it serves a valuable strategy unifying the company's vision and mission purpose.

A company's strategic plan lays out its future direction, performance targets and strategy. Development of a strategic vision, setting objectives, and crafting a strategy is the basic direction setting tasks of a company.

In this stage involves mapping out the company's direction that based on its short-term and long range performance targets and competitive moves and internal action approached, these can be used in achieving the targeted business results.

Crafting strategically constitute a strategic plan for coping with industry and competitive conditions, it is the expected actions of the industry's key players, challenges and issues that stand as obstacles to the company's success.

Structuring Strategic Decisions

The strategic structuring decisions are based inputs from a variety of assessments are relevant. Strategic decisions based on three types of assessments are outlined below:

The first stage is concerned organizational strengths and weaknesses.

Second stage is concerned evaluates the competitor strengths, weaknesses and strategies.

A third stage is concerned assesses the competitive context in the form of the customers and their needs, the market, and the market environment.

Stage 4: Implementing and Executing the Strategy

Managing strategy, implementation and execution of strategy is in operation oriented. It involves activity which aimed at shaping the performance of core business activities in a company. It is a supportive manner in a company. These things are eased and the most demanding to firms and it can be time consuming part of the strategy management and implementation process in firms. The strategic manager takes special initiative for converting strategic plans into actions and results and abilities to cope and direct organizational change, in this way motivates people, build and strengthen company competencies and competitive capabilities, create a strategy which work in better climate and either meet or beat standard performance targets in a company.

Managing strategy, implementation and execution of strategy process include the following principal aspects:
Trained and skilled staffing in the organization that consciously building and strengthening strategy supportive competencies and competitive capabilities and organizing the work effort in this achieve

strategy.

Development of budget that guide to company how to efficient utilization of ample resources into those activities critical to strategic success.

It ensures that policies, objectives and operating procedures, facilities rather than impede effective execution.

A company can be using the best known practices to perform core business activities and pushing for continuous improvement.

Installation information or software and operating systems which ensures to company personnel to better use and carry out their strategic roles day in and day out.

Motivating is the special tool to top level management of the company, it is useful to motivate their employees and to pursue the target objectively energetically.

Providing incentives and rewards to employees who have done excellent achievement, performance, objectives which is the output of better strategy execution.

Crafting culture of the company and its work climate conducive to successful strategy implementation and execution.

Exerting and internal leadership that's needed to drive for implementation forward and try to keep on improving strategy execution in the business. The organization has responsibility to take appropriate decisions on the basis of strengths, weakness of the firms.

Good strategy execution involves creating strong which is "fits" between strategy and organizational capabilities and executed by the skilled top level management in the enterprise, it is based between strategy and the reward structure. And also it is between strategy and internal operating systems, and between strategy and the organizational climate and culture in a company.

Stage 5: Monitoring Developments, Evaluating and Making Corrective Adjustments

Monitoring developments, evaluating and making corrective adjustments are one of the magnificent and significant stages in strategic management.

A company's strategy formulation, implementation and monitoring developments, evaluating and making corrective adjustments are never final; it is a continuous process for dramatic changes in terms of improvement.

An effective managing strategy is an ongoing process; it is not now and then the task of the company. It involves being evaluated the company's process, assessing the impact of new external developments and making corrective adjustments which relate to the company's vision, objectives, policies and execution of strategy into different methods in companies.

This stage decides whether to continue or change the company's mission and vision and objectives.

Company's strategist always gives directions relating to strategy which seem well to be matched industry and competition and performance targets are being met in this way strategist may decide to stay the course.

Well defined, planned and fine tuning strategic plan and continuing with ongoing efforts to improve strategy execution are sufficient in a company.

The company can be developing appropriate strategies and its directions which are coping and overcome encounters disruptive changes in its external environment.

Poor strategy monitoring impacts to the

company's business and reduce its operation efficiency in terms of profit, sales and customer base. For avoiding the poor strategy monitoring, a company must take corrective action when evaluation of strategy and try to avoid to poor monitoring and poor execution.

External and internal conditions of the company, a strategist reformulate a suitable strategy, to make proper objectives, mission, vision and policy and appropriate direction towards the growth and development of the company's performance in terms of competitive advantages and core competence.

A company ready and expected to modify changes its strategic vision, direction, objectives, and strategy over time in business. Proficient strategy execution provides an opportunity to firms for learning about new things, changes from the internal and external environment.

Well defined strategy execution and good assessment of company performance, which is needed for improving the company's normal and desirable results.

Strategy execution is continuously searching the dramatic changes for improvement in this way making corrective adjustments whenever and wherever a company is required.

Strategic Alternatives

Strategic alternatives are provided a magnificent role in planning perspective. Strategic alternatives always develop alternatives for strategy formulation, implementation and control of short term and long term planning perspective in companies.

CHAPTER 3
LONG TERM OBJECTIVES AND QUALITIES

INTRODUCTION

A company can set and formulate financial and strategic objectives. These objectives are based on the both the short-term and long term performance relating to business. Short term or annual objectives focus too and attention to delivering immediate performance improvement in the current year. Long term objectives focus on the long term prosperity of firm's or companies.

Long Term Objectives

Short run profit maximization is rarely based on the best approach to achieving sustained corporate growth and profitability of the firm. It is recognized by the strategic managers of the firm. Therefore, to achieve long term prosperity purpose strategic managers designed long term objectives.

Long term objectives of the firm or company or organization as listed below:

Profitability
Profitability is an important functional area of the long-term objectives of the firm. The ability of any business to operate in the long run depends on attaining on acceptable levels of profits. Strategically managed firms characteristically have a profit objective usually expressed in return on equity.

Productivity
Productivity is essential need for each strategist in the corporation. Strategic managers try to improve the productivity of their systems. Companies that can improve the input–output relationship normally increase profitability. Productivity objectives are sometimes stated in terms of desired decreases in most. This is an equally effective way to increase profitability.

Competitive Position
Competitive position can increase profitability and productivity of the company. Companies or firms or organization's Competitive position reduces the cost of production of the output. The corporate success depends on the firm's competitive position. It is strongly dominated in the market

Employee Development
It refers to experienced employees are the asset of the organization. For long-term purposes, the company's employees need training for further course of action that effectively and efficiently managed to produce productivity in the competitive position. Therefore, it is one of the major long-term objectives of the organization.

Employee Relationships
All companies actively seek good employee committed relations with organizational environment. The strategic manager should know the employee needs and expectations. Strategic managers take a decision to welfare program for the employees of the companies. It is only can improved of the employee's relationship with the organization.

Technological Leadership
Technological leadership can give a clear picture of the organization goals and objectives for the long term changes in the business scenario many companies state their objectives in terms of their technological leadership.

Public Responsibility
Business recognizes their social responsibilities towards to customer and

society. Public responsibility is build up long-term images in the society by through providing social work in public.

QUALITIES OF LONG TERM OBJECTIVES

Acceptable
Acceptable measures in companies are likely accepted by the strategic managers to pursue the objectives. Quality objectives are consistent with perceptions and the preference of the company mission and vision. Even if certain long term objectives are frequently designed to be acceptable to major interest groups external to the company.

Flexible
Long-term objectives should be modifiable in the event of the extraordinary changes due to environmental forecasts. At the same time, flexibility is usually increased at the expenses of specific events of the firms. Likewise, employee confidence may be tempered; therefore, an adjustment of a flexible objective may affect their job.

Measurable
Objectives must clearly and precisely measure in business. It clearly states what will be achieved and with what time frame. Objectives should measure because of

misunderstanding of long-term objectives of the company.

Motivating
Research studies indicate the people are most productive when objectives are set at a motivating level. This is the major problem for individuals and groups. Therefore, they are different in their perceptions of high enough. One valuable recommendation to strategic managers is to develop multiple objectives to motivating to individual and specific groups in the company.

Suitable
Long-term objectives are suitable to the broad aims of the organization or company. It clearly expressed in the statement of the company mission. Each objective should be a step toward attainment of the overall goals.

Understandable
Strategic mangers clearly understand at all levels in the organization for the accomplishment of objectives. They should understand major criteria for monitoring and evaluating of the organizational mission.

Achievable
It is the last long term quality objectives of the organization. Achievable strategies

always focus on the mission and vision of the organization or company. It is a very difficult task to strategist to face complex external difficulties in the business. Strategist designs a suitable strategy for implementation for the achievement of the goals and objectives of the company or firms or organization.

In totally Objectives should be quantitative, measurable, realistic, understandable, challenging, hierarchical, obtainable and concurrent among organizational units in the business.

Each objective can be associated with a time line in the company. Objectives generally stated in terms of growth of assets, sales volume, market share, diversification of business activities, earning per share and social responsibility towards the stakeholders of the company.

Clearly defined objectives are definitely brought excellent benefits to the company.
Objectives can be provided valuable and suitable direction, allow synergy, aid evaluation, establishes priorities, reduce uncertainty, minimize conflicts, stimulate exertion and aid in both the allocation of resources and the design of jobs in a company.

Short range objectives can be identical to long range objectives if an organization is already performing at the targeted long range level.

Short range objectives are related to the current year business trends, development of business policy within a year. Long term objectives will not be affecting the short term goals and objectives of the firm's.

Concept of Strategic Intent
When a company pursues ambitious strategic objectives and concentrates its full resources and competitive actions on achieving that objectives i.e. strategic intent exhibit in the company.

Company objectives sometimes play another role like signaling unmistakable strategic intent to make quantum gains in competing against key rivals and establish itself as a clear cut winner in the marketplace and enhance core competency and resources in the company.

It can be dominant in company within the industry in terms of unseating the existing industry leader, delivering the best customer service of any

company and turning a new technology into

products and services which capable of changing the way people work and live in the company.

Ambitious companies, strategic intent to be invariable due to proportion to their immediate capabilities and market positions.

The Need for Objectives At All Organizational Levels

The objectives are to be formulated by the top level management in all organizations.

Setting of objectives needs to be broken down into performance targets for each separate business, product line, functional department and individual work unit in the company.

Company performance can't reach full potential without clearly defined objectives in each area of the organization. It contributes directly to the desired companywide customs and results.

Strategic and financial objectives are set to performance targets for each organizational unit which support rather than conflict with or without negotiable the achievement of company.

CHAPTER 4
MICHAEL PORTER'S GENERIC STRATEGIES

INTRODUCTION
According to Michael Porter's, a choosing strategy in organizations which gains competitive advantage, it is choosing from three generic competitive approaches. They are as listed below:
Cost leadership/low cost
Differentiation
Focus

These strategies are known as generic because of all business or industries can pursue them regardless of whether they are manufacturing, service or not -for – profit organizations. Each of the generic strategy results from a company making consistent choices on product, market and distinctive competencies.

The product /market distinctive-competing

choices and generic competitive strategies at business level industries are listed below:

Cost leadership
Differentiation
Focus
And its choices as listed below:

Product differentiation
Market segmentation
Distinctive competency

Michael Porter's calls these strategies as generic strategies. Cost leadership strategy emphasizes to be producing standardized products at a very low per unit cost for consumers who are price sensitive. Differentiation strategy aims to be producing products and services which are considered unique in industry wide and directed towards to consumers who are relatively price insensitive.

Michael Porter's imply different organizational arrangements and make careful and proper control procedures and designed to be appropriate incentive systems for human resources in the enterprise.

In the case of the larger firms with greater accessibility of resources which typically compete on a cost leadership or differentiation basis.

In the case of smaller firms often compete on a focus basis in business.

Porter gives stresses to need for strategists to perform cost benefit analyses to evaluate the sharing opportunities which are existed among the company's and potential strategic business units. When sharing activities and resources that enhances competitive advantage by lowering costs or raising differentiation in company's. In additionally, prompting sharing, Porter stresses the need for company's to transfer skills and expertise among existing autonomous business units effectively in order to gain competitive advantage. These are depending upon the type of industry, size of the firm and the nature of competition, various strategies could yield major advantages in the form of cost leadership, differentiation, and focus.

COST LEADERSHIP STRATEGIES

A company's goal in pursuing a cost leadership or low cost strategy is to out perform competitors by doing everything. It can to pursue goods or service at a cost lower than their competitors. Cost leadership strategy is required strategies choice of product and service into different market segments and its competitors. It pursued in conjunction with differentiation. Cost leadership strategies are gaining to forward, backward and horizontal integration strategies. A successful cost leadership strategy usually utilization of the entire firm's in the form of higher efficiency, low overhead, limited perks to human resources, minimize the waste, intensive screening of the budget and its tools like income and expenditure, effective using the wide span control, rewards linked to cost containment, and broad employee participation in cost control efforts in the firm's in this reduce the cost of the product and services.

Advantages of Cost leadership Strategy

There are two advantages occurring from cost leadership strategy. They are as mentioned below:

Cost leadership strategy refers to lower costs of product and service offered by the company, the cost leader is able to charge a lower price than its competitors. The cost leader makes a higher profit than its competitors because of its lowers costs of products and service.

If industry rivalry increases and companies start to compete on price, the cost leader will be able to withstand competition start to compete on price; the cost leader will be able to withstand competition better than other companies because of its lower costs. For both reasons, cost leaders are likely to earn above–average profits.

Disadvantages of Cost Leadership Strategy
Important disadvantages of cost leadership strategy are outlined:
The principal dangers of the cost–leadership approach risk in competitors ability to find ways of producing at lower cost and beat the cost leader.

Competitor's ability to easily imitate the cost leader's method is another threat to the cost leadership strategy. The cost leadership strategy carries a risk that the cost leader, the single-minded desire to reduce costs, may lose right to changes in customer tastes.

Strategic Choices
The company cost leader strategy is choosing a low level of product differentiation. Differentiation is expensive for the company; if the company expands resources to make its product unique than its costs rise. The cost leader aims for a level of differentiation not marketing inferior to that of the differentiator (a company competes by spending resources on product development) but a level obtainable at low cost.

The cost leader also normally ignores the different market segments and positions. Its product is to appeal to the average customer. The main reason is that the cost leader makes it choice by developing a line of products and tailored to the needs of different market segments. It is an expensive proposition. A cost leader normally engages to only a limited amount of market segmentation. Customer happy when the company normally charges a lower price than its competitors attracts customers to its products and service.

In developing distinctive competencies, the overriding goal of the cost leader must be to develop competencies. It enables to increase its efficiency and lower its costs compared with its competitors. The development of distinctive competencies in manufacturing and material management is central to achieving this goal. Companies are pursuing a low cost strategy may attempt to ride down the experience therefore; they can lower their manufacturing costs. Achieving a low cost position may also require that the company develop skills in flexible manufacturing and adopt develop skills in flexible manufacturing and adopt efficient materials -management techniques.

DIFFERENTIATION STRATEGY

Differentiation strategy refers to the differentiated company's ability to satisfy a customer need. A differentiation strategy should be pursued only after a careful study of buyer's needs and prefer to determine the feasibility of incorporating one or more unique product features. It helps company to charge a premium price; a price considerably above the industry average. The company's ability to increase by charging premium prices (rather than by reducing costs of the output) allows the differentiator to outperform its competitors and gain above average profits. The premium price is usually substantially above the price charged by the cost leader, and customers pay it therefore, they believe the product-differentiated qualities to be worth the difference. Successful differentiation provides greater product flexibility, greater compatibility, lower costs, improved services, less maintenance, greater convenience or more features in this strategy.

Advantages of Differentiation Strategy

Advantages of differentiation strategy as outlined:
The company's unit price must be higher than that of the average company and its unit cost must be equivalent to that of the average company.

The company's unit must be lower than that of the average company and Its unit price must be equivalent to that of the average company, The company must have both a lower unit and a higher unit price than the average company.

Disadvantages of Differentiation Strategy
Major disadvantages of differentiation strategy are listed below:

Developing the distinctive competency needed to provide a differentiation advantage is often expensive to company.

A differential cost usually has higher costs than the cost leader. The main problems with the differentiation strategy center on the company's long-term ability to maintain its perceived uniqueness in customers' eye on the market.

A differentiation strategy is the ease to competitors can imitate a differentiator product and the difficulty of maintaining a premium price.

Strategic Choice of Differentiation Strategy
The differentiate strategy chooses a high level of product differentiation to gain a competitive advantage. Differentiation can

be achieved with quality, innovation and responsive a product appeal to customers' psychological desires can become a source of differentiation. A company pursues a differentiation strategy strives to differentiate itself along as many dimensions as possible. The less it resembles its rival, the more it is protected from competition, and the wider is its market appeal.

A differentiator chooses to market segment. The company offers a product to design for each market differentiator, but a company chooses to serve just niches where it has a specific different advantage.

A differentiated company concentrates on the organizational function that provides the source of its differentiation advantage. Differentiation based on the innovation and technological competency depends on R&D function. A differentiator does not want to increase costs unnecessarily.

FOCUS STRATEGY

Focus strategy is the third generic competitive strategy and one of the foundations of business level strategy. Focus strategy is directed towards serving the need of a limited customer group or segment. A focus strategy is the focused company concentrates on serving a particular market niche that may be defined geographically, by type of customer, or by segment of the product line. A successful focus strategy depends on an industry segments like customer, product line, geographical segment.

Once a company has chosen its market segment, a company may pursue a focus strategy through either a differentiation or a low cost approach. A focused company is a specialized

differentiator or cost leader. Because of their small size, few focus firms are able to pursue cost leadership and differentiation simultaneously. If a firm uses a low cost approach, it competes against the cost leader in the market segment where it has no cost advantage with focus strategy, a company concentrates on small volume custom products, where it has a cost and leaves the large volume standardized market to the cost leader.

If a focused pursues a different approach, then all the means of differentiation that are open to the differentiators are available to the focused company. The point is that the focused company competes with the differentiator in only one or in just a few segments. Focused companies are likely to develop differentiated product qualities successfully because of their knowledge of a small customer set or knowledge of a region. Furthermore, concentrating on a small range of products. Sometimes allows a focused to develop innovations faster than a large differentiation. A focused company concentrates on building market share in one market segment and, if successful, may begin to serve more and more market segments.

Advantages of Focus Strategy

An important advantage of focus strategy as listed below:

Focus strategy is protected from competitors to the extent therefore; it can provide a product or service.

The focus strategy gives the focused power over its buyer therefore; they cannot get the something from anyone also It permits a company stay close to its customers and to respond to their changing needs.

It can be developed superior skills in customer responsiveness, it's based unit's ability to serve the needs of regional customer.

These are advantages are focused on efficiency, quality, innovation and customer responsiveness of the company.

Disadvantages of Focus Strategy

An important and major disadvantage of focus strategy is listed below:

Key focuser failure due to powerful suppliers of goods and service. Therefore, the competitor is strong control of market segmentation.

A large differentiator sometimes is not experience to focus strategy due to the difficulty of managing a large number of market segments.
A focuser produces at a small volume, its production costs often exceed. Higher cost can also reduce profitability and even loss of the business. So that this factor has one of important disadvantages of focus strategy.

The focuser's in niche can suddenly disappear because of technological changes in customer tastes.

Focuser is not concentrated of efficiency, quality, innovation and customer responsiveness, Its impact is to failure of focus strategy in a company.

Strategic Choices of Focus Strategy
The specific product/ market/ distinctive competency choice is made by a focused company. Differentiation can be high or low because the company can pursue a low-

cost or differentiation approach. As for customer groups, a focused company chooses specific niches in which to compete, rather than going for the whole market, like the cost leader. A focuser may pursue any distinctive competency because it can pursue any kind of differentiation or low cost advantage.

A focused strategy company can take to develop a competitive advantage explain why they're so many small companies in relation to large ones. A focused company has enormous opportunity to develop its own niche and compete against low cost and differentiated enterprises, which tend to be larger. A focus strategy provides an opportunity for an entrepreneur to find and then exploit a gap in the market by developing an innovative product that customers cannot do without.

Generic Strategies Comparative Skills and Resource Requirement

Generic strategies comparative skills and resource requirement are presented below:
Overall Cost Leadership Commonly Required skills and Resources
Sustained capital investment and easily to access capital.
Business process engineering skills.
Intensive supervisions of labor in firm's.
The low cost distribution system is existed in

firms.

Overall Cost Leadership Common organizational Requirement
Tight cost control in the firms.
It required frequent and detailed control reports.
It structured organization responsibilities.
Incentives based on meeting strict quantitative targets.

Differentiation Commonly Required skills and Resources
Strong marketing abilities in firms.
Product engineering in business.
Creative flair in firm's.
Strong capability in basic research in firm's.
Corporate reputation for quality or technological leadership.
Low tradition in the industry or unique combinations of skills drawn from other business.
Strong cooperation from channels in business.

Differentiation Common organizational Requirement
Strong coordination among function likein R&D, product development, and marketing
Subjective measurement and incentives instead of quantitative measures.
Amenities to attract highly skilled labor,

scientists or creative people in business.

Focus Commonly Required skills and Resources
It is the combination of the above policies directed towards particular strategic target

Focus Common organizational Requirement
It is the combination of the above policies directed towards the particular strategic targets

Best Cost Provider Strategy
Best cost provider strategy is the new model. It is the further development of three generic strategies. The five competitive generic strategies are coming under the best cost provider strategy model. This model is being pursued competitive advantage in business.

The Five Competitive Generic Strategies
The five generic competitive strategies are outlined:
Overall Low cost leadership strategy
Broad Differentiation strategy
Focused Low – Cost Strategy
Broad cost Provider Strategy
Focused Differentiation Strategy

CHAPTER 5
GRAND STRATEGIES STRUCTURES IN ENTERPRISE'S

INTRODUCTION

A firm's uses various strategy alternatives for achieving its growth, survival objectives. Grand strategies are also called as a master or business strategies that are intended to provide basic direction for strategic actions. The grand strategies aim is the long term sustainable development and growth of the organization.

Grand strategies indicate how long range objective will be achieved. Thus, grand strategy can be defined as a comprehensive general approach that guides major actions.

Grand strategies serve as the basis for achieving major long term objectives of a single business; concentration market,

market development, product development, innovation, horizontal integration, vertical integration, joint venture, concentration diversification, conglomerate diversification, retrenchment, turn around, divestiture and liquidation. Grand strategies are usually combined all strategies of the organization or company arena.

A grand strategy principally consists of stability strategies, expansion strategies, retrenchment strategies and combination strategies. These strategies are known as grand strategies or master strategies or direction strategies.

Features of Grand Strategies
The basic features of grand strategies are outlined:

Stability Strategy Basic Feature
Stability strategy refers to maintaining the status quo of the existing business operation. Stability strategy aims at a slow growth rate
It can be maintained the existing level of efforts in business.
It is satisfied with incremental growth of its functional performance in terms of its customer groups, customer functions.

Expansion Strategy Basic Feature
An organization desired to expand extents its

business network widening the scope of its customer groups, customer functions and state of the art.

Expansion Strategy Basic Feature
technologies. Intensive expansion is a fundamental approach to safeguard and develop the organizations product market and there by increased the volume of scales, profit, market share and total business network very rapidly. It can be entering new businesses that are unrelated to existing businesses.

Retrenchment Strategy Basic Feature
An organization decides to reduce its business operation by reducing the scope of customer groups or customer functions or alternative technologies with a view to have better control for better performance, retrenchment strategies are accepted.
It can be dropped the business as such through sell out or liquidation.

Combination
Combination strategy refers to the combination of the stability, expansion and retrenchment strategy in different levels of the organization

CHARACTERISTICS AND SCOPE OF VARIOUS GRAND STRATEGIES

Stability Strategy

Stability strategy refers to maintaining the status quo of the existing business operation. Stability strategy aims at a slow growth rate. It follows as a matter of principle when an organization attempts incremental growth of its functional performance in terms of its customer groups, customer functions, and alternative technologies, whether in combination or individually. Thus when an organization decides to serve the same target customer groups with same products service and follows the same objective to maintain the stable business status, it can be termed as stability strategy.

Characteristics of Stability Strategy

A firm opting for a stability strategy maintains with the same business, same product marked posture and functions, maintaining the same level of effort as at status quo of the existing business.

It aims to enhance functional efficiencies in on achievement way, it is achieved through better deployment and utilization of resource.

It involves the assessment of the firm which is maintaining the status quo in terms of desired income and profits.

It can be helped to business to incremental improvements in functional efficiencies.

Generally, this strategy will be quite modest in business growth objectives; it is applicable only firms which modest growth objective will vote for this strategy.

This strategy is a safety oriented and status quo oriented strategy. It does not require much fresh investment. It is fairly frequently employed strategy in business.

Firm's which have followed this strategy, these firm's are definitely expected benefits from concentrating its resource and attention towards the existing business/ products and markets. And the rewards are also limited in firms.

Stability strategy does not permit the firm's renewal process for bringing in fresh investments and new products and markets for the firm.

EXPANSION STRATEGY

When an organization desired to expand extents its business network widening the scope of its customer groups, customer functions and state of the art technologies, we have the making of an expansion strategy. Expansion or growth strategy is principally adopted when an organization enhances its level of objectives with high target. Intensive expansion is a fundamental approach to safeguard and develop the organizations product market and thereby increased the volume of scales, profit, market share and total business network very rapidly.

Characteristics of Expansion Strategy

Expansion strategy is just opposite to stability strategy.

Expansion strategies are those strategies which are highly rewarded in firms and also the risk is too high in business.

It is flexible and most frequently employed generic strategy.

It is the true growth strategy; the firm's aims of expanding business activities in this way to meet its growth objectives in firms.

It involves the redefinition of the business activities of the company.

It requires fresh investments and it involves the process of renewal of the firm in this way introducing new business / products /markets are facilitated only by expansion strategy.

It is highly versatile strategy; it offers several permutations and combinations for growth. For this purpose, the firm's opting for the expansion strategy can generate many alternatives within the strategy by altering its propositions regarding in terms of products, markets, functions and pick the one that suits it most.

It has failed two major routes; intensification and diversification.

Intensification and diversification are the tool of growth strategies; it pursues difference it's actually growth in business. Firm's intensification strategy pursues growth by working its current business operation in businesses.

Intensification can be encompassed with the three alternative routes as outlined;
Market penetration strategy
Market development strategy
Product development strategy

Diversification strategy refers to the expansion of business into new businesses that are outside the current businesses and markets. An important type's diversification as listed below:
Related diversification Unrelated Diversification Internal Diversification External Diversification Horizontal Diversification Vertical Diversification Active Diversification Passive diversification

Concentric Diversification

Vertically integrated diversification involves that firm's are going into new businesses which are related to current ones.

Vertical integration further classified into two broad components such as forward integration and backward integration.

The firm's remain vertically within the given

product process sequence; it is intermediaries in the chain become new businesses.

Concentration diversification refers to introducing new products which are connected to the firm's existing process or technology. Therefore, the new products are not vertically linked to the existing ones. They are not considered as intermediates.

They serve new functions in new markets and it is spinned off from the firm's existing facilities.

Conglomerate diversification refers to a new business is added to the firm's portfolio. It is unrelated diversification and it disconnected from the existing business operation of firm's in the form of process / technology / function. In this strategy, there is no connection between the existing business and new business.

RETRENCHMENT/ DIVESTMENT STRATEGY

When an organization decides to reduce its business operation by reducing the scope of customer groups or customer functions or alternative technologies with a view to have better control for better performance, retrenchment strategies are accepted. In retrenchment strategy, unattractive and unwanted areas of business are sequenced gradually. It is not a matter of failure of business planning, rather well planned exercise to get rid of unprofitable parts of a business which will help the organization concentrate its total attention on the most profitable and promising areas of business only.

Characteristics of Retrenchment/ Divestment Strategy

It involves retrenchment of some of the activities in a given business of the firm or sells out of some of the business assets.

It is one of the corporate strategies to reduce its operation by reducing the scope of customer groups and customer functions.

It involves the redefinition of the business operation.

Compulsions in this strategy are different and vary in business operation.

Retrenchment is necessary in the following firm's conditions:

When business unprofitable

When high competition from the competitor

When an industry is over capacity

When failure of strategy

COMBINATION STRATEGY

The changing business environment, an organization may also find it beneficial to adopt a unique combination of stability, expansion and retrenchment in different levels related areas of business which depending on the business environment. In other words, combination strategy refers to the combination of the stability, expansion and retrenchment strategy in different levels of the organization

Major Reasons for Organizations Adopting Different Grand Strategies

A firm's has adopted a stability strategy in the following conditions:

It is less risk, it involves less change and people feel comfortable with things which are happening in firms.

The business environment relatively stable condition.

Expansion of business is threatening to firm's.

Firm's consolidation required through stabilizing after a period of rapid expansion of business operation.

A firm's adopted Expansion strategy in the following conditions:

It's imperative when the environment demands increase the pace of activity in a firm's operations.

It is the results of expanding business operation in firms; chief executive is the responsible person for the firm's growth.

Increase the size of business operation which is control over the market vis – a – vis competitors.

It is advantageous to firm's in this way enhancing the scale of operations.

Firm's adopted Retrenchment strategy in the following conditions:
When the management no longer wishes to remain in business both partly or wholly due to continuing losses and unviable.
When business environment could be faced threaten to firm's operations.
It can be ensured to be a reallocation of resources from unprofitable to profitable business.

Firm's Combination Strategy is adopted in the following conditions:
An organization is large and ready to face complex environment in business operations.
An organization is consisting of different businesses, each of which comes under the different industry that requiring a different response.

PRODUCT MARKET EXPANSION GREED

Expansion or growth strategy can either be via intensification or diversification. Product market expansion greed developed by Igor Ansoff gave framework as presented that explained the intensification options available to a firm.

Product Market Expansion Greed

I. Growth in existing product markets
Increased market share Increased product usage Increase the frequency used Increase the quantity used
Find a new application for current users

II. Product development
Add product features, product refinement
Develop a new generation product
Develop new product for the same market

III. Market development Expand geographically
Target new segments

IV. Diversification involving new products and new markets
Related
Unrelated

Market Penetration
Market penetration strategy is the one most important expansion strategy of the current business. The firms direct its core resources to the profitable growth of a single product. It is in a single market and with a single technology.

Market Development
Market development is consisting of marketing present's products and services which offered by company, company is

required to be adding different channels of distribution or by changing the content of advertising or promotional media.

Product development
It involves substantial modification of existing products and services or creation of new, but these are related items that can be marketed to current customers through established channels.

CHAPTER 6
DIVERSIFICATION

INTRODUCTION
Diversification refers to a company is diverting the business focus from the existing traditional areas to new promising areas. Since technology is changing day by day, 'customer' demands are changing accordingly. The company introduced new and substitute products and service available in the market to meet the customer's expectations and to draw their attention. These are changing attitudes of the customers, the company has opened more and more new areas of promising business. Diversification may involve internal or external, related or unrelated, horizontal or vertical, active or passive dimensions. The change of business focus may be either in terms of customer function, customer group and new alternative technologies.

Types of Diversification

An important type's diversification as listed below:
Related diversification
Unrelated diversification
Internal diversification
External diversification
Horizontal diversification
Vertical diversification
Active diversification
Passive diversification
Concentric diversification
Conglomerate diversification

Related Diversification

Related diversification is diversification into a new business activity that is linked to the company's existing business activity normally these activities are commonly between one or more components of each activity's of existing business activity of value chain. Normally these linkages are based on manufacturing marketing or technological commodities.

Related diversification options for manufacturer in business as outlined:
Exchange or Share assets or competencies, thereby exploiting the following:
Brand name of company Marketing skills of company Sales and distribution capacity

Manufacturing skills.
R&D and new product capability.
Economies of scale for company's products and services.

Unrelated Diversification
Unrelated diversification is diversification into a new business area that has no obvious connection with any of the companies existing areas. Unrelated diversification options for a manufacturer as outlined:
Manage and allocate cash flow in the company
Obtain high rate of investment in the company Obtain for bargain price
Refocus a firm
Reduce risk of operating in multiple product markets
Tax benefits
Obtain liquid assets in the company
Vertical integration of company
Defend against a takeover in firms.

Internal diversification
Diversification business activities within the company such is known as internal diversification. It means that a company ready to introduce new products in the same geographical areas.

External Diversification
External diversification involves to

diversification of the business activities like manufacturing, products, marketing, technological changes diversified with the other companies to save for the operating costs of the goods and service.

Horizontal Diversification
Horizontal diversification is undertaken in order to increase market share by expansion of the same product lines with more varieties to serve customers in different areas, of different types and affluence levels. Horizontal diversification may be taken up to expand business geographically into new territories by taking up an increase market share and improve business volume.

Vertical Diversification
Vertical diversification means diversification into a new production line to produce items required as inputs for other main products of the same company. Vertical integration refers to company diversify its business into a number of different business areas. Diversification into a new production line to produce goods and service required as inputs for other main products of the same company. For instance a company diversifies its business into a number of different business areas like banking and financial services, energy and utility, health care and

insurance, manufacturing retail, telecom. It may be undertaken by a company with the purpose of either maintaining continuous flow of products and service to customers. The Vertical Integration Company offers numerous products and service for satisfying customers. A company is opening its own sales and marketing division and showrooms for selling product and service to customer instead of selling through agents and distributors. It can be controlled over the input supply and output distribution also. Vertical integration further classified into two broad categories. They are listed below:
Backward or Upstream integration
Forward or Downstream integration

Upstream or backward Integration
Back integration or upstream refers to the company is diversifying the business operation towards some of the raw materials or input supply. Backward integration involves moving into intermediate manufacturing and raw material production.

Downstream or Forward integration
Forward integration or downstream refers to the company is diversifying business operations for marketing sales distribution of products and services and taking up these activities to bring the organization closer to the ultimate customer.

The stages in the raw material to customer production chain. It indicates the four steps are listed below:
Intermediate manufacture
Assembly
Distribution
Ultimate customer
Backward integration involves moving into intermediate manufacturing and raw material production. Forward integration involves movement into distribution. At each stage in chain, value is added to the product. It means that a company at that stage takes the product produced in the previous stage, transforms it in some way and then sells the output at a higher price to a company at the next stage in the chain. The difference between the price paid for inputs and the price at which the product is sold is a measure of the value added at that stage.

The value added concept, consider the production chain in the personal computer industry. This indicates that the computer industry. Raw materials companies include the manufacture of specialty ceramics, chemicals, and metal such as Dow Chemicals and Union Carbide. These companies sell their output to the manufacturers of intermediate products the intermediate manufacturers include companies like Intel and Motorola, transform the ceramics, chemicals and metal they purchase into computer components such as microprocessors, memory chips, and disk drives. In doing so they add value to the new materials, they purchase. These components are then sold to assembly companies like Apple and Compaq, which take these components and transform, them into personal computers i.e., add value to the components they purchase many of the completed personal computer world, which in turn sell them to final customers. The distribution also value added to the product by making it accessible to customers, and by providing service and support thus value is added by companies at each stage in the raw materials to consumer chain.

Viewed this way, vertical integration involves a choice about which value added stages of raw material to consumer chain to compete in.
A company achieve full integration what it produces all of a particular input needed for its possessor when it disposes of all of its inputs through its own operations.

Taper integration occurs when a company buys from independent suppliers in addition to company-owned suppliers or when it disposes of its output through independent outlets in addition to company owned outlets.

Creating Value through Vertical Integration

A company pursuing vertical integration is normally motivated by a desire to strengthen the competitive position of its original or core business. There are four vital arguments for pursuing a vertical integration strategy. They are as listed below:

Enables the company to build barriers to new competition,

Facilitates investments in efficiency–enhancing specialized assets.

Protects product quality Results in improved scheduling.

Enables the Company to Build Barriers to New Competition

The company's vertical integrating backward to gain control over the source of inputs and distribution channels. A company can build effective distribution channels for distribution of products and service. The company builds barriers to new entry into its industry to extend to apply to this strategy effectively to avoid competition. Therefore, thereby enabling the company to charge a higher price and make greater profits.

Facilitating Investments in Specialized Assets

A specialized asset is an asset that is designed to perform a specific task and whose value is significantly reduced in its next best use. A specialized asset may be a piece of equipment or skills. The skills acquired by the companies or individuals through training and experience. Companies and individuals invest in specialized asset because these assets allow them to lower the costs of value creation and to better differentiate their product offering from that of competitors, thereby, facilitating premium pricing. These specialized assets use very specialized purposes.

Companies always invest in specialized equipment because it enables it to lower its manufacturing costs and increase its quality. Secondly it invests in developing highly specialized technological knowledge because it develop better products than their rivals. Therefore, specialization can be achieved a competitive advantage at the industry level.

A company may find it very difficult to persuade other companies' in adjacent stages in the raw material to consumer production chain to undertake investments in specialized assets. As a result, companies or individuals are to realize the economic gains associated with investments. It may have to vertically integrate into such adjacent stages and make the investment itself.

Protecting Product Quality
The companies' main aim is protecting product quality. Vertical integration enables a company to become a differentiated player in its core business. If a company is the integration, therefore it can protect product quality without affecting standard ness of the product quality.

Improved Scheduling
Strategic advantages arise from the easier planning, coordination and scheduling of adjacent processes. It made possible in vertically integrated organizations or companies can be particularly important in companies trying to relate the benefits of just in time inventory systems.

DISADVANTAGES OF VERTICAL INTEGRATION
Cost Disadvantages
Cost is the main factor of the company to gain a production cost advantages. Meanwhile vertical integration can raise costs, if a company becomes committed to purchasing inputs from company owned suppliers when low cost external sources of supply exist. Company owned might high operating costs compared with the independent suppliers.

Technological Changes

Technological changes are other disadvantages of the vertical integration. When technology changes fast and outdated its plants and equipment. Therefore, it is also major disadvantages of the company.

Demand Uncertainty
It can also be extremely risky in unstable or unpredicted demand condition. In this case, it is very difficult to achieve their activities in the company.

Others
Vertical integration poses problems of balancing capacity at each stage in the value chain.
Integrating forward or backward often calls for radically different skills and business capabilities.
Backward vertical integration into the production of parts and components can reduce a company's strength.

CONCENTRIC DIVERSIFICATION
Concentric diversification is to concentrate the direction of business for expansion and diversification is to concentrate the direction in the same and attendant product lines. Concentric diversification may take the form of marketing related or technology related diversification.

Active diversification is the long-term expansion of the business activities. Passive diversification is the short term and negative impact of continuity of long term contracts with partners.
The concentration diversification, the business is linked to the company existing business through its process, technology and marketing.

The new product is only connected in a loop like manner at one or more points in the company's existing process or technology or product chain.

Conglomerate Diversification
It refers to the new businesses or products are disjointed from the existing businesses or products in every way;
It is a totally unrelated diversification.
In process or technology or function, these are no connection between the new products and the existing ones.
It is no common thread at all with the company's present position.

Creating Value through Diversification
Most companies first consider diversification when they are generating financial resources, therefore, it is excess to maintain to competitive advantage in their original or core business. The diversified company can

generate value in three main routes. They are listed below:

Acquiring and restructuring
Transferring competencies
Economies of scope

ACQUIRING AND RESTRUCTURING

Acquiring and restructuring involved with acquiring and restructuring poorly run enterprises. A restructuring strategy rests on the presumption that an efficiently managed company can create value by acquiring inefficient and poorly managed enterprises and improving their efficiency. This approach can be considered diversification because the acquired company does not have to be in the same industry as the acquiring company for the strategy to work. Improvements in the efficiency of an acquired company can come from a number of sources. They are listed below:

The acquiring company usually replaces the top management team of the acquired company with more aggressive top management team.

The new top management team is encouraged to sell off any unproductive assets like executive jets and elaborate corporate headquarters and to reduce staffing levels.

The new top management team is also

encouraged to intervene in the running of the acquired business to seek out routes of improving the unit's efficiency, quality, innovativeness, and customer responsiveness.

To motivate the new top management team and other employees of the acquired unit to undertake such actions, increases in their pay may be linked to industries in the performance of the acquired unit.

The acquiring company often establishes performance goals for the acquired company.

Transferring Competencies

The company's diversification strategy of transferring competencies seeks out new business related to their existing business by one or more value creation functions, for instance, manufacturing, marketing, materials management and R&D. They want to create value by drawing on the distinctive skills in one or more of their existing value creation function in order to improve the competitive position of the new business. It can improve the efficiency of their existing business.

Economies of Scope

It arises when two or more business units share resources like;

Manufacturing facilities

Distribution channels

Advertising

R&D costs

Each business unit utilized their capacity better and reduced to operating cost.

RETRENCHMENT, DIVESTMENT AND LIQUIDATION STRATEGY

When an organization decides to reduce its business operation by reducing the scope of customer groups or customer functions or alternative technologies with a view to have better control for better performance, retrenchment strategies are accepted. In retrenchment strategy, unattractive and unwanted areas of business are sequenced gradually. It is not a matter of failure of business planning, rather well planned exercise to get rid of unprofitable parts of a business which will help the organization concentrate its total attention on the most profitable and promising areas of business only.

These things are done through an attempt to find out the problem areas and diagnose the causes of the firm's problems.
Once identified the problems, firms will be taken the next steps to solve the problems.
This result is to search different type's retrenchment strategies in businesses.
For retrenchment process, a firm will be selected and adopted at turnaround strategy.
And also adapt to the divestment strategy to

reduce functional activities in firms.

If none of these actions cannot be worked, that time a firm can be chosen to abandon the activities totally in terms of liquidation strategy.

TURNAROUND STRATEGY

Many companies restructure their operations divesting themselves of their diversified activities, because they wish to focus more their core business area. An integral part of the restructuring, therefore, it is the development of strategy for turning around the company's core or remaining business areas.

In this section, we shall review in some detail the various steps to be taken by companies in turnaround troubled business areas. We shall first look at the causes of corporate decline and then discuss the main elements of successful turnaround strategies.

Retrenchment can be done either internally or externally infirm. Internal retrenchment which takes into place that is emphasis to lay on improving its internal efficiency which is known as a turnaround strategy.

There are certain conditions or indicators are the main reasons for turnaround is

needed to firm's have for survival, growth, development and increased profitability. The major danger signs in the industry are listed below:
Persistent negative cash flow in business
Negative profits in business
Declining market shares of firm's
Deterioration in physical facilities in business.

Over manning, high turnover of employees and low morale of human resource in firm's.
Uncompetitive products and services in industry. Mismanagement is the main reason in a firm.

The Causes of Corporate Decline
The seven causes are an important of the corporate decline. They are listed below:
Poor management
Over expansion
Inadequate financial controls
High costs
New competition
Unforeseen demand shifts
Organizational inertia

Poor Management
Poor management involves a multitude of sins; it is ringing from sheer incompetence to neglect of core businesses and an insufficient number of good managers. Therefore, these things are not necessarily a bad thing.

Research study showed that in the presence of a dominant and an autocratic chief executive with a passion for empire building strategies characterizes involved for many failing companies.

Over Expansion
Rapid expansion and extensive diversification, these diversifications tend to be poorly conceived and adds little value to a company much diversification its result is loss of control and inability to cope with recessionary conditions. Moreover, companies expand rapidly their business involves large amounts of debt financing. Adverse economic conditions can limit a company's ability to meet its debt requirements and can they precipitate a financial crisis.

Inadequate financial controls
It is the common trend of the business. Financial manager is a failure to assign profit responsibility for the financial consequences of their actions, it can encourage to mid-level managers to employ excess staff and spend resource beyond what is necessary for maximum efficiency of the company.

High Costs
Inadequate financial control can lead to high

costs. Its common cause like low labor productivity and management has failed to introduce new labor saving technologies and high rate of wages for employees. These are an important factor for companies competing on costs in the global market and have a failure to realize economies of scale, therefore, it results impact on companies low market share.

New Competition

New competition is essential to companies for competition in the industrial world. A company ready to tackle competition from rivals. Because of new technology made huge cutthroat competition and increase in productivity at low cost of output. Many companies have failed because of unable to face threats of competitors. Therefore, new competition kills idle companies in the business world.

Unforeseen Demand Shifts

Environment threat like marketing, technology, political, social, legal, cultural environment can change open market opportunities for new products. Its consequence is the unforeseen demand shifts from old to new products. Therefore, the customer has preference to buy new product at a low cost. When companies fail to fulfillment of the above fact then have a failure in the business world.

Organizational Inertia
The emergence of powerful new competition and unforeseen shifts in demand might not be enough to cause corporate decline. Organization is slow to respond to environmental changes.

Main Elements of Successful Turnaround Strategies
The main steps of turnaround strategies for success of companies' business. They are listed below:
Changing leadership
Redefining strategic focus
Asset sales and closures
Improving profitability
Acquisitions

Changing the Leadership
Old leadership had failure, new leader is an essential element of retrenchment and turnaround situation to resolve the crisis, to motivate lower level managers, listen to the views of others and delegate power when appropriate.

Redefining Strategic Focus
It refers to redefining company's strategy for restructuring of business. It is identifying the business in the portfolio which has the

best for the company for long-term profit and growth prospects and concentrating investment there.

Assets Sales and Closures
Having redefined its strategic focus, a company should divest as many unwanted assets as it can find buyer for and liquidate whatever remains. It is important not to confuse unwanted assets within profitable assets.

Improving Profitability
Improving profitability involves a number of steps to improve efficiency, quality, innovation and customer responsiveness. It involves the following issues:
Layoffs white and blue collar employee
Investments in labor saving equipment
Assessment of profit, it is responsibility to individuals and subunits within the company, by a change of organizational structure if necessary.
Tightening financial controls
Cutting back on marginal products
Reengineering business process to cut costs and boost productivity and
Introducing total quality management.

ACQUISITIONS
Turnaround strategy involves making an acquisition primarily to strengthen the

competitive position of a company's remaining core operations.

Issues for Successful Turnaround Strategies

Turnaround strategies are to be successful because of successful issues which are related to firm's imperative focus on the short-term and long term financing needs as well as strategic issues which are suitable to make a workable action plan for a turnaround with firms are listed below:

Analysis of product, market, production processes, competition and each market segment positioning.

Strategic manager clear thinking about the marketplace and production logic.

Proper implementation of plans of target setting, and get feedback and take right remedial action.

Contributory Elements for Turnaround in Firm's

Changes in top level management in business
Initial credibility building actions in firm's
Neutralizing external pressures
Initial control
Identifying quick payoff activities
Quick cost reductions
Revenue Generations
Asset liquidation for generating cash
Mobilizations of the organizations Better

internal coordination

DIVESTMENT/CUTBACK STRATEGY

It involves the sale and disposing off or shedding business units or product divisions or segments of business operations to reinvest the resources for other production and potential business purposes.

Divestment is usually a part of revival, rehabilitation and restructuring plan attempted when a turnaround strategy becomes unsuccessful.

The strategy in the case may be to sell off a part of business or products, or giving up the control over a subsidiary or a demerger so that the wholly owned subsidiaries may be floated off as an independent organization.

Organization maybe choose to divest in two ways: a part of the organization may choose to divest by way of serving its financial and managerial control and separating it as an independent organization for all purposes. Alternatively, an organization may sell a unit outright for which marketing strategy should be proven.

The basic objective underlying organization unit may be hindrance on the total profitability and growth, particularly when opportunities of strategic alternative investment exist. So, divestment may be a sensible positive strategic decision and not due to helpless condition. Further there may be other types of strategies like business level strategy, functional level strategy, annual strategy, grand strategy, and corporate strategy.

Reasons to Adopt Divestment Strategy in Firms

A business had been acquired which proves that to be mismatched and cannot be integrated within the company.

Persistent financial problems which create the negative cash flows from a particular business operation in a company which is to be needed for divestment of that business.

Firm unable to cope to severity of competition from rival firms; it may cause to divest business operations.

Technology up gradation is required, in this case, the firm able to survive but where it is possible for the firm to invest in it, a firm preferable option would be taken for divest business operations.

A better alternative which may be available for investment that causing a firm to divest a part of its unprofitable businesses in a firm's operations.

Liquidation Strategies

Retrenchment strategy is considered the most and extreme and unattractive is liquidation strategy; it involves closing down a firm and selling its assets.

It is considered as the last resort because which leads to serious consequences like loss of employment for workers and other employees, termination of opportunities where a firm can pursue any future activities and the stigma of failure.

In India, many small firms like small scale units, proprietorship firms and partnership ventures are liquidated frequently but medium and large sized companies rarely liquidate in India.

The company management, government, banks and financial institutions, trade unions, suppliers and creditors and other agencies are extremely reluctant to take decisions or ask or formulate suitable policy for liquidation.

Selling assets for implementing a liquidation strategy, it will be difficult to sell and difficult to find buyers for assets of liquidation firm. In this case, the liquidation firm cannot be expected adequate compensation from selling the assets which are treated scrap by buyers.

Liquidation – the Strategy of Last Resort
Sometimes a business crisis is too far gone

to salvage or is not worth salvaging given the resources it will take and its profit prospects. Closing a crisis-ridden business down and liquidating its assets is sometimes the best and wisest strategy of all strategic alternatives. Liquidation is the most unpleasant and painful because of the hardships of job eliminations and the effect of business closings in local communities. Therefore, in hopeless situations, an early liquidation effort usually serves owner- stake holder interests better than an inevitable bankruptcy.

End Game Strategies

End game strategy steers a middle course between pressuring the status quo and existing as soon as possible.

An end game strategy is a reasonable strategic option for a weak business in the following circumstances:

When the industry's long-term prospectsare attractive.

When rejuvenating the business would be too costly or at best marginally profitable.

When the firm's market share is becoming costly to maintain or defend.

When reduced levels of competitive effort will not trigger an immediate or rapid falloff in sales.

When the enterprise can redeploy the freed

resources in higher opportunity areas.

When the business is not a crucial or core component of a diversified company's overall lineup business

When the business does not contribute other desired features to a company's business portfolio.

ABOUT THE AUTHOR

Dr.B. Hiriyappa, is a Ph.D, He is a prolific author of 16 books: Strategic Management, Strategic Management for Chartered Accountant, Investment Management, Organizational Behavior, business environment, Business Policy and Strategic Management, Strategic Management and Business Policy : For Managers and Consultant.25 E books are Strategic Analysis, Strategic Planning, Formulation of Functional Strategy, Business Environment, Business Policy and Strategic management etc.

www.ingramcontent.com/pod-product-compliance
Lightning Source LLC
Chambersburg PA
CBHW031531210526
45464CB00012B/2442